SAINTS
Tell Their Stories

BY PATRICIA MITCHELL
ILLUSTRATED BY MARIA CRISTINA LO CASCIO

Contents

The Saints

Every saint has a different story to tell. Some have bravely died for their faith. Others have worked very hard to help the poor. From all over the world men, women, and even children have become saints. But the saints, as different as they are, all have something in common: they loved God above everything else, and they served him in whatever way he called them.

This book features twenty-six saints who will tell their story to you. You will recognize some of them, but others you may not know very well. Listen carefully, because they all have something important to teach you.

Saints have been honored since the beginning of the church. People throughout the ages have looked to them as friends and guides, since they show us how to grow closer to Jesus. And, just as you might ask a friend to pray for you, people have asked the saints to pray for them and to go before God with their concerns and requests.

So go ahead and ask the saints to pray for you. After all, you're all part of the same family—the family of God!

The Blessed Virgin Mary

Born: unknown date, Palestine
Feast Days: birth on September 8, Annunciation on March 25,
Assumption on August 15

Imagine my surprise when an angel appeared to me one day and told me that I would be the mother of God's Son! I was frightened but also very honored when the angel said to me, "Hail Mary, full of grace."

What do you think I said to the angel after he delivered his message? "I am the Lord's handmaiden. Let everything happen just as you said."

When the angel visited me, I was engaged to Joseph, and we were making plans to get married. I knew that Joseph would be very surprised and upset when he realized that I was going to have a baby. But guess what? God took care of everything. In a dream, an angel told Joseph to go ahead and marry me because the baby was God's Son.

I loved Jesus so much! When he grew up, I listened to his teachings and saw him perform many miracles. I was so sad when he died on the cross, but then three days later I saw him again, alive! He had risen from the dead.

Sometimes we don't understand what God is doing in our lives. But when we say yes to him, he does wonderful things. See what he did for me.

St. Joseph

BORN: UNKNOWN DATE, PALESTINE
FEAST DAYS: MARCH 19, MAY 1

I was an ordinary carpenter, living in Nazareth in Galilee and engaged to Mary. Then an angel told me in a dream that the baby Mary was carrying was going to be very special, and that I would help raise him.

After Jesus was born, I had another dream. An angel told me to take Mary and Jesus and flee to Egypt because King Herod wanted to kill Jesus. We had to leave Nazareth and live in Egypt until the angel told me it was safe to return home.

Jesus and I spent lots of time in my workshop, where I taught him how to work with wood. He was a fast learner. I'll never forget the time we went to Jerusalem for Passover. Jesus was twelve years old. We lost him, and spent three days trying to find him. Then we discovered him in the Temple, listening to the teachers and asking them questions.

I didn't live long enough to see Jesus complete his mission. But I had completed mine—to care for Jesus. God has a mission for you, too. Just pray and listen—he'll tell you what it is, and he'll help you do it.

St. John the Baptist

Born: unknown date, Palestine
Feast Days: June 24, August 29

My name is John, and I am Jesus' cousin. And like Jesus, my birth was also announced by an angel. My dad, Zechariah, and my mom, Elizabeth, were older and still had no children. One day while my father was serving in the Temple, an angel told him he would have a son who would prepare the way for the Lord.

After I grew up, I went to live in the wilderness. Many people came to visit me. I proclaimed God's message to them: "Be sorry for your sins, for the kingdom of heaven is at hand." Then I baptized them in the River Jordan. I also told them that someone greater than me was to come, who would baptize them with the Holy Spirit. I was talking about Jesus!

One day Jesus came to the river to be baptized. I said, "Here is the Lamb of God!" Then I heard a voice from heaven saying, "This is my beloved Son, with whom I am very pleased."

You are God's son or daughter, and he is very pleased with you! He is so happy when you come to him in the Sacrament of Reconciliation, and he is so eager to forgive your sins and give you his grace.

St. John the Apostle

Born: unknown date, Palestine
Feast Day: December 27

Everyone loves good news. The word "gospel" means goods news, and I wrote the gospel that has my name, the Gospel of John.

My story is also in the gospel. I was a fisherman with my brother James when we first saw Jesus and decided to follow him. We saw such amazing things. Jesus turned water into wine, healed people of diseases, and multiplied the fish and loaves. Once I climbed a mountain with Jesus and saw him shine like the sun. I was also at the foot of the cross with Jesus' mother when Jesus was crucified. That was a very sad day.

But three days later, Peter and I went to Jesus' tomb and found it empty. Jesus had risen from the dead! I spent the rest of my life telling others about my friend, Jesus. I said, "God loved the world so much that he sent us his Son. Everyone who believes in him will live forever!"

Yes, that's the good news. God is love. When you look at the cross, it will help you remember how much God loves and cares for you and how much he wants to be with you, both now and forever.

St. Luke

Born: unknown date, Antioch, Turkey
Feast Day: October 18

Have you ever sailed on a ship? I went on many sea voyages with my traveling companion, Paul. We were on a mission: to spread the good news about Jesus everywhere we went. One time we were shipwrecked, but God saved us from harm!

I wrote two books of the Bible. One is a gospel that bears my name, the Gospel of Luke, and it's all about Jesus. In my gospel, you can read about Jesus' parable of the prodigal son. He told that story to show us how much our heavenly Father loves us, even when we have done wrong, and how he wants to forgive us and welcome us back into his family of love.

The Acts of the Apostles, the other book I wrote, is filled with many exciting adventures, beginning with Pentecost when the Holy Spirit came upon all the disciples and gave them the courage to preach the good news. The story of our shipwreck is also in Acts.

I was a physician, but I'm also called an evangelist because I told others about Jesus. You can be an evangelist, too. Just tell everyone you know how wonderful it is to have Jesus as your best friend!

St. Peter

BORN: UNKNOWN DATE, PALESTINE
FEAST DAYS: FEBRUARY 22, JUNE 29

Do you want to hear how I met Jesus? I had just been fishing with my brother Andrew, but we hadn't caught any fish. We were washing our nets by the shore of the lake, and along came Jesus. He said to me, "Lower your nets for a catch." I was doubtful we'd catch anything—after all, we'd been fishing all night. But I did what he said, and guess what? There were so many fish in the net that it started to break. I knew this was a miracle, and it scared me. But Jesus said, "Do not be afraid. From now on you will be fishing for people."

Jesus called me the "rock," and said he would build his church on me. I loved Jesus so much and told him I would never deny him, but after his arrest, I did deny him—three times. I was so sorry, and he forgave me. And I did become the "rock," the first pope to lead the church.

Isn't it amazing? God used me, even though I had once denied him. That just goes to show you that you don't have to be perfect to be a follower of Jesus. You just have to say yes, like I did!

St. Paul

BORN: UNKNOWN DATE, TARSUS, TURKEY
FEAST DAYS: JANUARY 25, JUNE 29

Pharisees were Jews who wanted to follow all of God's laws perfectly. I was a Pharisee, and I thought I was following God's laws when I put Jews in prison who believed in Jesus.

One day I was going to Damascus to round up more of Jesus' followers. Suddenly I was blinded by a great light, and I heard a voice who said I was persecuting Jesus. It was Jesus himself! For three days, I couldn't see, but then a man named Ananias came to pray with me, and my sight was restored.

I was baptized and became a follower of Jesus. I traveled all over the world to share the good news about Jesus. I went wherever the Spirit led me. I helped set up Christian communities in many far-off places, including Rome. Sometimes my preaching caused disturbances, and I was beaten and thrown in prison. I wrote many letters to these communities from prison.

Eventually my letters became part of the Bible. In these letters, I told the people that God gave us not just a set of rules to follow but his very self through his Son, Jesus. Jesus lives in our hearts. What a difference that made in my life!

St. Stephen

BORN: UNKNOWN DATE, PALESTINE
FEAST DAY: DECEMBER 26

In the early days of Christianity, the apostles were very busy praying and preaching. They needed someone else to distribute food to the widows each day, and so they chose me and six other men to do the job.

When I wasn't distributing food, I was talking about Jesus and praying with people. Some of the Jewish leaders didn't like what I was saying, and they spread lies about me. I was seized and brought before the Jewish council. I didn't try to defend myself. Instead I explained how Jesus was the One the prophets had spoken about who would come to save his people.

The Jewish leaders refused to listen to me. Then they became so angry that they dragged me out of the city and began to stone me. As I looked up to the heavens, I saw Jesus standing next to the Father. Today I am honored as the first Christian to die for Jesus.

Just before I died, I prayed, "Lord, do not hold this sin against them." I forgave my persecutors, just as Jesus had done. It's difficult to forgive people when they hurt us. But we can forgive when we ask the Holy Spirit for the grace to do so.

St. Nicholas

BORN: C. 270, PATARA, LYCIA, TURKEY

FEAST DAY: DECEMBER 6

I was the bishop of Myra in the early days of the church. There are many stories about me. One says that I appeared and calmed a storm, saving a ship from sinking.

But I'm especially known for my generosity. For example, I once helped a man who had three daughters. He was a very poor nobleman, and he could not pay for his daughters' weddings. The man was very sad because he thought he would have to sell his girls into slavery. When I heard about the man, I took a bag of gold and, during the night, I threw it into his window. No one saw me. I did the same thing the next two nights. Finally the man found out who I was. I made him promise that he would tell no one about my deed until after I had died.

My gifts to the family inspired the tradition of giving gifts on my feast day, December 6, and on Christmas. That's why Santa Claus is also known as St. Nicholas! But remember, the greatest gift we could ever have is Jesus. When he lives in our hearts, we want to be as generous to others as he has been to us.

St. Alban

BORN: 3RD CENTURY, VERULAMIUM, ENGLAND
FEAST DAY: JUNE 22

I lived in England when it was ruled by the Roman Empire and, like other Roman citizens, I worshiped the Roman gods.

One day I took pity on a Catholic priest who was on the run from the Roman authorities. I hid the priest in my home. When I saw how he prayed and how he talked about Jesus, my heart was stirred and I became a believer.

Soon the soldiers were approaching my house to seize the priest. I said to him, "Give me your clothes. Escape through the back door, and I'll pretend to be you."

But my plan was discovered, and the Roman guards arrested me. I was condemned to death, and the guards accompanied me to the nearby hill where I was to be beheaded. On the way, we had to cross a river. When I lifted my eyes to heaven, the river immediately dried up so that we could cross over to the other side.

When the executioner saw this miracle, he also converted to Christ. He refused to kill me, and another person beheaded both of us.

What a great gift it is to have faith and believe in Jesus! Ask the Holy Spirit to strengthen your own faith. He will do it.

St. George

BORN: 3RD CENTURY, NICODEMIA, TURKEY
FEAST DAY: APRIL 23

I was an army general in charge of five thousand men. I fought for the Roman emperor, Diocletian. I had to lead my men into battle and inspire them to fight for the emperor.

Then one day the emperor ruled that every soldier in his army had to worship the Roman gods. I was a Christian, and I wasn't about to worship other gods, so I resigned.

Several years later, the emperor decided to ban gatherings of Christians and destroy churches. I traveled to the imperial court and asked the emperor to change his mind. It didn't work. He tortured and beheaded me.

There are many stories about me. You may have heard that I killed a dragon to rescue a princess. I am often pictured on a horse, slaying the dragon. But it wasn't for slaying a dragon that I was made a saint but because I stood up to the emperor. Sometimes we have to be brave and stand up for what's right. And when we need courage, we can pray. Jesus gave me courage, and he will give it to you, too, whenever you ask for it!

St. Martin of Tours

BORN: 316, SAVARIA, HUNGARY
FEAST DAY: NOVEMBER 11

One cold wintry day I met a beggar on the street. He didn't have anything warm to wear, so I cut my cape in two and gave him half. That night in a dream I saw Jesus wearing the cloak. I was so surprised! Soon after I was baptized.

Even though I had been a soldier in the Roman army for many years, one day I decided I wanted to leave and become a soldier for Christ. My commander was angry with me and called me a coward. So I promised to stand unarmed during the next battle, with only Jesus to protect me. But the following day, the enemy unexpectedly surrendered, and I was able to leave the army.

Eventually I founded the first monastery in Western Europe and also became bishop of the city of Tours in France.

God showed me that he wanted me to work for him, not for the Roman army. If you pray and grow close to God, his Holy Spirit will show you what he wants you to do with your life. Just trust in him, as I did. He loves you, and he won't let you down!

St. Jerome

BORN: 347, STRIDON, CROATIA
FEAST DAY: SEPTEMBER 30

Do you like to learn new languages? When I was a teenager, I went to Rome to study language and grammar. Then one day while I was ill, I had a vision of Jesus. He challenged me to become his disciple. So I went into the desert to fast and pray, and I learned the Hebrew language.

That really helped me because I spent the rest of my life translating the Bible from the Hebrew language into Latin. The church used this translation for hundreds of years. I also wrote about many different Bible passages.

Later I went to live in the Holy Land, where many of the stories in the Bible take place. There are also stories about me. One says I pulled a thorn out of a lion's paw because the creature was in so much pain. So I am often pictured with a lion.

I just loved reading and praying through the Bible. I often said, "If you don't know the Bible, you don't know Christ." You can really get to know Jesus when you read stories about him in the gospels and imagine yourself there with him. Try it yourself and see!

St. Patrick

BORN: 389, GREAT BRITAIN
FEAST DAY: MARCH 17

When I was a teenager, I was captured by pirates and sent to Ireland to work as a slave. I missed my family terribly, but as I tended sheep in the fields, I prayed and grew close to God. One day six years later, I heard God telling me to escape, so I found a ship to take me home.

Then I had a dream that a man came from Ireland carrying a bundle of letters. The letters were the voices of the Irish, begging me to return. I realized that God had kept me safe in Ireland so that I could return there to become a missionary and build his church.

I went to Ireland as a bishop and taught people about God using a shamrock. Just as the shamrock has three leaves but one stem, so God is three Persons—Father, Son, and Holy Spirit—but one God.

As you can see from my life, sometimes bad things happen to us. But God is always with us, and he can turn bad things into good ones. I didn't like being a slave in Ireland, but God used me to share the good news of his love to the Irish people.

St. Boniface

BORN: C. 673, CREDITON, ENGLAND
FEAST DAY: JUNE 5

When I was growing up, many people had still not heard about Jesus, and they worshiped other gods. After I became a monk in my own country of England, I was sent to Germany to tell the people there about the true God.

When I arrived, I discovered that the people worshiped a gigantic oak tree dedicated to Thor, the god of thunder. I had to show them that Thor was a false god, so I decided to cut down the tree.

But God helped me. I had just started to swing the axe when a sudden blast of wind crashed the tree to the ground. The people were so amazed that they listened to my message about Jesus. They decided that *he* was the true God.

I spent the rest of my life in Germany and established churches all over that country. One day as I was preparing for an outdoor Mass, I was martyred.

How blessed we are to worship such an awesome and mighty God! You can worship the true God when you pray and go to Mass. Jesus is present in the Eucharist—his true Body and Blood. He is so pleased when you receive him in Holy Communion.

St. Francis of Assisi

BORN: 1181, ASSISI, ITALY
FEAST DAY: OCTOBER 4

I wasn't born into a poor family—in fact, my father was a rich merchant. But I decided to become poor, just like Jesus

When I was young, I joined the army and fought many battles. But then God spoke to me. "Who can do more for you," he asked, "the lord or the servant?" I knew that God was the Lord and that I should serve him.

So I left the army and lived a simple life. Other men joined me and together we preached the gospel. We loved all of God's creatures, especially the animals and birds. Once I even tamed a wolf.

One day when I was praying in the run-down church of San Damiano in Assisi, I heard God tell me to "repair my church." Later I realized that God wanted me to repair more than one church building. He wanted me to rebuild his entire church by sharing the message of his love. Over the years, many people have become Franciscans and helped to build up God's church.

I was the richest of poor men. I was poor, but because Jesus loved me, I was rich! You are rich, too, no matter how much money your family has, if you know and love Jesus.

St. Anthony of Padua

BORN: 1195, LISBON, PORTUGAL
FEAST DAY: JUNE 13

One day some Franciscan monks visited the monastery in Portugal where I lived. They were going to Africa to preach the gospel. When I learned later that they had been killed for their faith, I wanted to go to Africa, too.

So I left Portugal, but I got so sick on my trip that I had to return. On the way back, my ship ran into a storm and was blown off course. I landed in Italy, where I worked in the kitchen of a monastery.

One day some visitors came to the monastery for a celebration, and I was called upon to preach to them. Everyone loved my sermon, so I was sent all over Italy and into France to preach. Many came to hear me.

Once when I was in Padua, the people didn't want to listen to me. Instead they made fun of what I was saying. So I turned to a river and preached to the fish. To everyone's amazement, the fish lifted their heads above the water as if to listen while I spoke.

I had a gift for preaching. We all have gifts that God can use to build his kingdom. Ask the Holy Spirit to help you discover your gifts.

St. Ignatius of Loyola

BORN: DECEMBER 24, 1491, LOYOLA, SPAIN
FEAST DAY: JULY 31

As a soldier, I fought in many battles. One day a canon ball badly injured my leg. I had to undergo painful operations and, while I was recovering, I was given books to read about the life of Christ and the lives of the saints.

I was so excited by all that I read that I gave up my sword and armor and decided to give my life to God.

The next year I spent time praying. I asked the Virgin Mary to help me know what I should do for God. I also wrote my Spiritual Exercises, a set of meditations and prayers that are still used today to help people love God more and listen to what he is saying to them.

I decided to go back to school, and there I met six companions. Together we formed the Society of Jesus. As a group, we vowed to serve the church in whatever way the pope asked us. We started many colleges around the world and trained many men for the priesthood. Today there are thousands of Jesuits all over the world, teaching and preaching God's word.

Isn't it amazing what we can do when we come together to work for God's glory?

St. Innocent

BORN: AUGUST 26, 1797, IRKUTSK, RUSSIA
FEAST DAYS: MARCH 31, OCTOBER 6 (ORTHODOX CALENDAR)

Icy water splashed over the bow of the canoe as I battled the waves in the stormy ocean. I was on yet another trip to islands off the Alaskan coast to visit members of my far-flung diocese.

As a Russian Orthodox priest, I had moved from my home in Irkutsk, in the depths of Siberian Russia, to preach the gospel in the wilderness of Alaska. It took me a year to get there. I had many exciting adventures. I had to travel by kayak, dog sled, and even reindeer through harsh wintry conditions to get to the Aleutian Islands.

With help from the local people I was able to build a church. I learned six local languages and translated portions of the Bible for the people. Eventually I decided to become a monk. Then I became bishop of a huge diocese that spread from mainland Russia to my beloved Aleutian Islands.

God's family is made up of people from all over the world. Sometimes we seem different on the outside because of our language, customs, or the way we look. But on the inside, we're all the same because we're all one in Christ.

St. John Bosco

BORN: AUGUST 16, 1815, CASTELNUOVO, ITALY
FEAST DAY: JANUARY 31

My father died when I was only two years old, and my family was poor. Once, while working as a shepherd boy, I dreamed that I was surrounded by boys who were fighting and misbehaving. A man with a kindly face said that I would have to control the boys not by beating them but with kindness.

When I became a priest, I moved to the city of Turin. There I visited some boys in prison. I was shocked at how badly they were treated. So I decided to help the boys that lived in the streets. Many of them were wild and unruly.

But I didn't get angry or impatient with them. Instead, I treated them as Jesus would, with love, kindness, and encouragement. I also played games with the boys. We had so much fun! I started a school, and my mother helped me care for them.

Other priests joined me, and we became the Salesian Society, named after my favorite saint, Francis de Sales. Now there are Salesian communities all over the world. My dream had come true!

Jesus wants us to treat everyone with love and kindness, no matter who they are. And when we do, we show them how much Jesus loves them, too.

St. Bernadette

BORN: JANUARY 7, 1844, LOURDES, FRANCE
FEAST DAY: APRIL 16

I was only fourteen years old when the Virgin Mary first appeared to me in Lourdes, France.

I had been sent out to fetch firewood near my home. As I bent down, I heard a rustling noise and looked up to see a beautiful young woman dressed in white with a blue sash and a golden rose on each foot.

During one of these apparitions, the young woman told me to drink water from the spring under the rock.

"I don't see a spring," I said to her. "The ground is dry." But when I dug into the soil with my hands, water flowed freely.

I saw Mary eighteen times. I was questioned by officials from the church and the French government many times about these apparitions. I told them that Mary wanted a chapel built at the site of the spring. Since then, millions of people have visited Lourdes and many have been healed by bathing in the waters from the spring.

Why was I chosen to see Mary? I can't tell you but I do know that God uses even children to build his kingdom! Look how he used me.

St. Thérèse of Lisieux

BORN: JANUARY 2, 1873, ALENÇON, FRANCE
FEAST DAY: OCTOBER 1

I was the youngest of five girls. My mother died when I was only four, and my older sisters helped raise me. But first one sister, and then another, left home to become a nun at the nearby convent in Lisieux.

I also wanted to become a nun at the convent, but first God had to change me because I was too sensitive. One Christmas Eve I overheard my father say something about me that could have hurt my feelings, but this time it didn't. After that, I wasn't so sensitive. I called this my Christmas miracle.

When I was fifteen, I entered the convent. I wanted to show God how much I loved him, but I was only a young nun and couldn't do great things like the missionaries. Then I realized I could offer God little acts of love each day. For example, I could decide not to complain or I could smile at sisters who were irritable. I called this my "little way."

I died of tuberculosis when I was only twenty-four, but my "little way" became very famous through the story I wrote about my life. What little things can you do today to show Jesus how much you love him?

St. Frances Xavier Cabrini

BORN: JULY 15, 1850, SANT'ANGELO, ITALY
FEAST DAY: NOVEMBER 13

Even as a little girl, my heart was set on going on a mission to China. But God had other plans for me!

I was the youngest of thirteen children, and growing up I was often sick. Because of my poor health, I was refused entry into two communities of sisters. So I worked as a teacher in an orphanage. Then I founded my own community, the Missionaries of the Sacred Heart. With the pope's blessing, I opened two convents in Rome. But instead of sending me to the Far East, where I wanted to go, the pope sent me to the far West— New York!

In New York, where I was known as Mother Cabrini, I raised money for a house to use as a convent and orphanage. Our sisters opened many more hospitals, convents, orphanages, and schools in eight different countries. I became a citizen and the first American to become a saint.

Sometimes we think we can't do great things for God. On our own we can't, but the Holy Spirit can help us do anything. Even my poor health didn't stop God from working in me. He gives us the strength we need to do his will.

St. Maximilian Kolbe

BORN: JANUARY 7, 1894, ZDUNSKA WOLA, POLAND
FEAST DAY: AUGUST 14

When I was a child, I had a vision of Mary that made me want to be her "knight" so that I could fight evil in the world. I became a Franciscan priest and started a religious magazine that was very popular. I also worked with other Franciscans to start a radio station and college. During World War II, I spoke out against the Nazis and hid Jewish people that the Nazis were trying to kill. Eventually I was arrested and sent to a terrible concentration camp called Auschwitz. Here's what happened:

"A prisoner has escaped!" declared the commandant. "Now ten of you must die as punishment."

As the chosen prisoners were being marched away, one cried out, "My wife and children—I will never see them again!"

So I stepped forward. "Let me take his place," I said.

Almost three weeks later, I was still alive in a starvation cell. I had encouraged the others by praying with them and singing hymns. Finally the guards put me to death with an injection of poison.

I died peacefully, knowing that I had laid down my life for another man, just as Jesus on the cross had laid down his life for me. And like Jesus, I had fought evil with love.

Blessed Pier Giorgio Frassati

BORN: APRIL 6, 1901, TURIN, ITALY
FEAST DAY: JULY 4

Do you like sports? I loved skiing and mountain climbing. But even more, I loved God. And I loved helping God's people, especially those who were poor.

My father was a wealthy newspaper owner, and I used any pocket money he gave me to help those less fortunate. I often had to walk home because I had given away my train fare. One day a poor mother and her son came to the door to beg. "I see you have no shoes," I said to the boy. So I gave him mine.

There were so many poor people in my city. I had to make sure they had food to eat, a place to sleep, and clothes to wear. This kept me busy, but I also went to Mass each day and prayed. And I found time to ski and climb mountains with my friends.

When I was twenty-four years old, I came down with a disease called polio and died. My parents were surprised at how many people came to my funeral. They were all the poor people whom I had helped.

You can help poor people, too. Maybe you can give them some of your allowance, or bring some food to a soup kitchen.

Blessed Mother Teresa of Calcutta

BORN: AUGUST 27, 1910, SKOPJE, MACEDONIA
FEAST DAY: SEPTEMBER 5

I was fascinated by the lives of the missionaries, so when I was eighteen, I joined the Sisters of Loreto and moved to India.

I loved my work teaching young girls, but on a train trip God spoke to me. He wanted me to start a new order of sisters called the Missionaries of Charity who would work with the poorest of the poor—all those people who are unwanted, uncared for, and unloved.

So I went by myself to work in the slums of Calcutta. Many sisters joined me, and we opened houses all over the world to care for the very poor and dying. We lived very simply, like the poor we served.

I often told people how important it is to respect life. Everyone is loved by God, from unborn babies to the homeless people who are living in the streets. Every life is precious.

I used to tell people, "Do something beautiful for God." It can be something simple, like being kind to your family or visiting someone who is lonely. Remember, when you love and serve others, you are really loving and serving Jesus!

59

Index of Saints

Alban, 3rd century, Verulamium, England

Anthony of Padua, 1195, Lisbon, Portugal

Bernadette, January 7, 1844, Lourdes, France

Boniface, c. 673, Crediton, England

Frances Xavier Cabrini, July 15, 1850, Sant'Angelo, Italy

Francis of Assisi, 1181, Assisi, Italy

George, 3rd century, Nicodemia, Turkey

Ignatius of Loyola, December 24, 1491, Loyola, Spain

Innocent, August 26, 1797, Irkutsk, Russia

Jerome, 347, Stridon, Croatia

John the Apostle, unknown date, Palestine

John the Baptist, unknown date, Palestine

John Bosco, August 16, 1815, Castelnuovo, Italy

Joseph, unknown date, Palestine

Luke, unknown date, Antioch, Turkey

Martin of Tours, 316, Savaria, Hungary

The Blessed Virgin Mary, unknown date, Palestine

Maximilian Kolbe, January 7, 1894, Zdunska Wola, Poland

Nicholas, c. 270, Lycia, Turkey

Patrick, 389, Great Britain

Paul, unknown date, Tarsus, Turkey

Peter, unknown date, Palestine

Pier Giorgio Frassati, April 6, 1901, Turin, Italy

Stephen, unknown date, Palestine

Mother Teresa, August 27, 1910, Skopje, Macedonia

Thérèse of Lisieux, January 2, 1873, Alençon, France

Published in 2009 in the U.S. and Canada by
The Word Among Us Press
7115 Guilford Drive
Frederick Maryland 21704
www.wau.org

ISBN: 978-1-59325-161-1

First edition 2009
Fourth printing 2012

Text based on the original by Christopher Doyle
Copyright © 2009 Anno Domini Publishing
www.ad-publishing.com

Text copyright © 2009 Patricia Mitchell
Illustrations copyright © 2009 Maria Cristina Lo Cascio
Publishing Director Annette Reynolds
Editor Nicola Bull
Art Director Gerald Rogers
Pre-production Krystyna Kowalska Hewitt
Production John Laister

Printed and bound in Malaysia
August 2012